Beautiful Street
An Adult Coloring Book

Copyright © 2021Robber Fickle
All Rights Reserved.

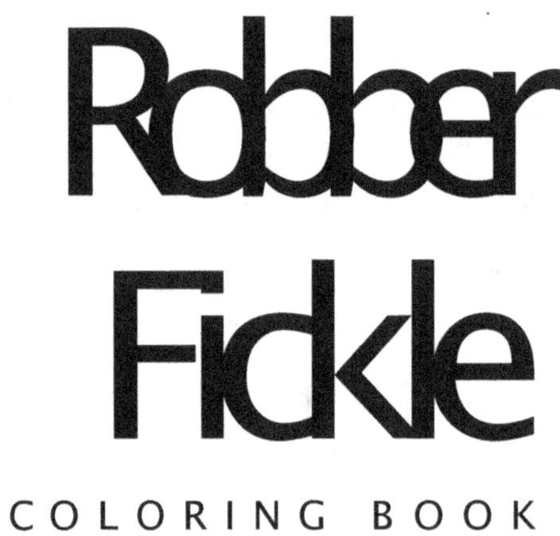

For Any Question and Suggestions
robberfickle@gmail.com

This Book Belongs To

....

TELEPHONE

COFFEE HOUSE
OFFICE CENTER
CENTRAL SHOP
SUPERMARKET
SALE
SALE
SALE

TELEPHONE

TELEPHONE

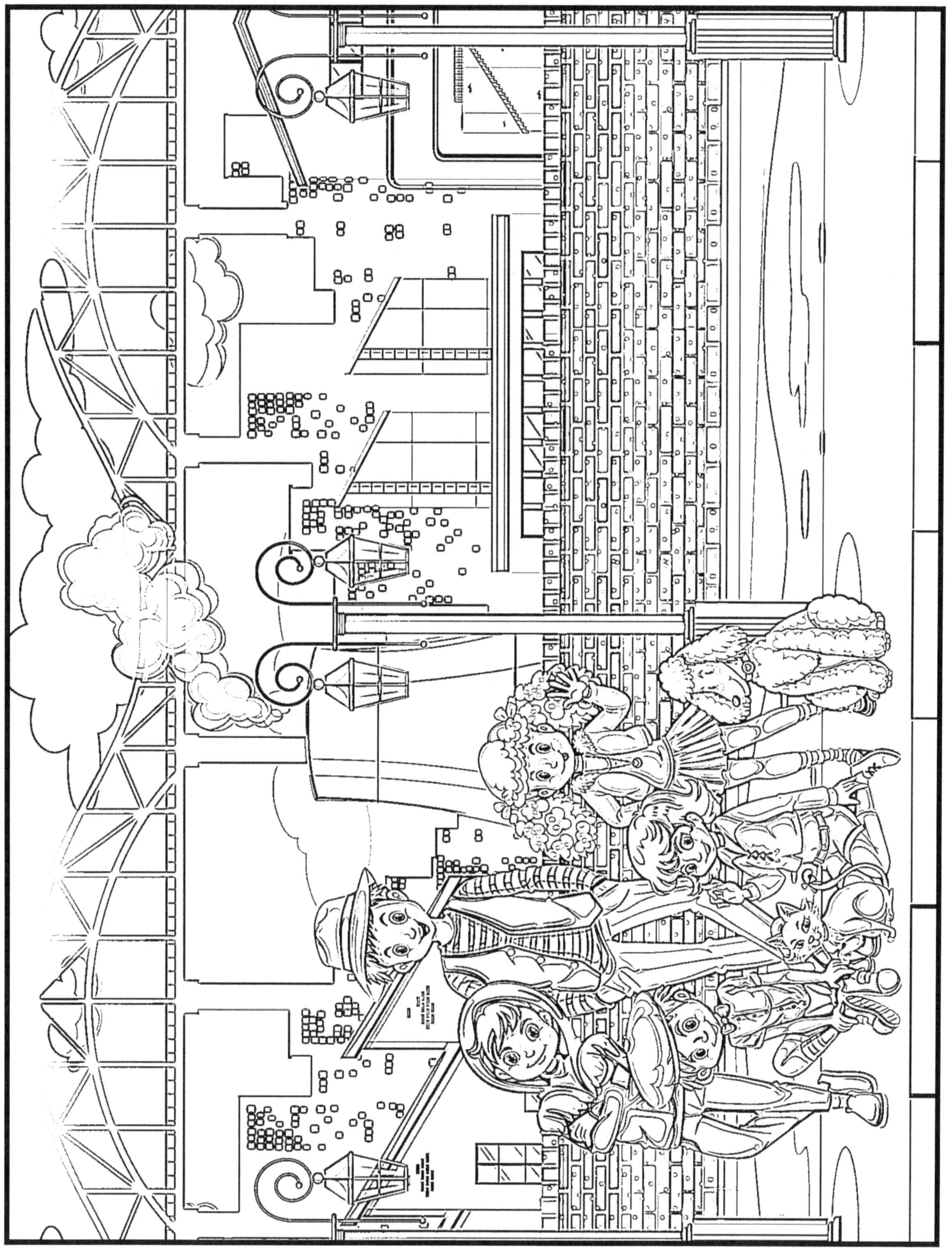

TELEPHONE

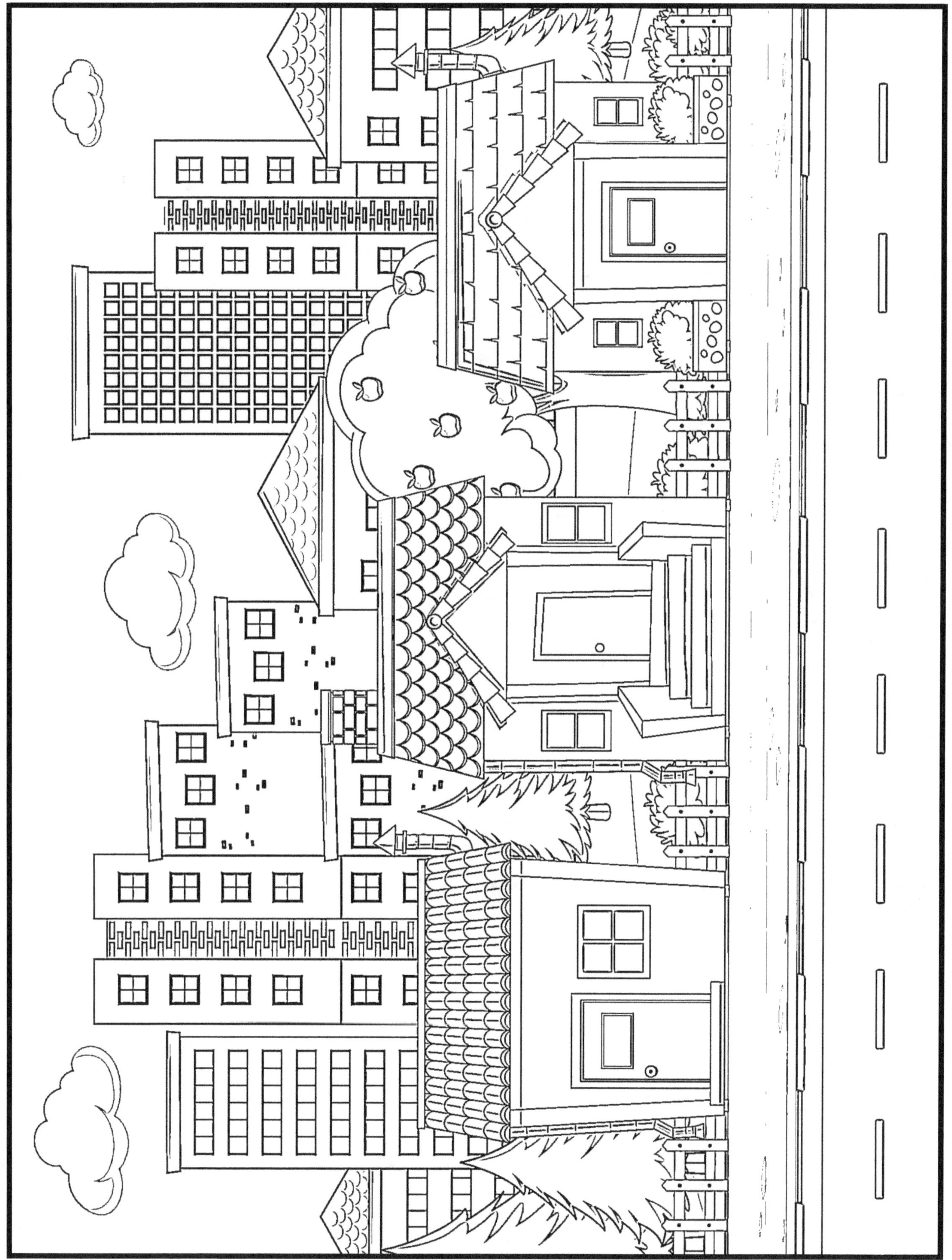

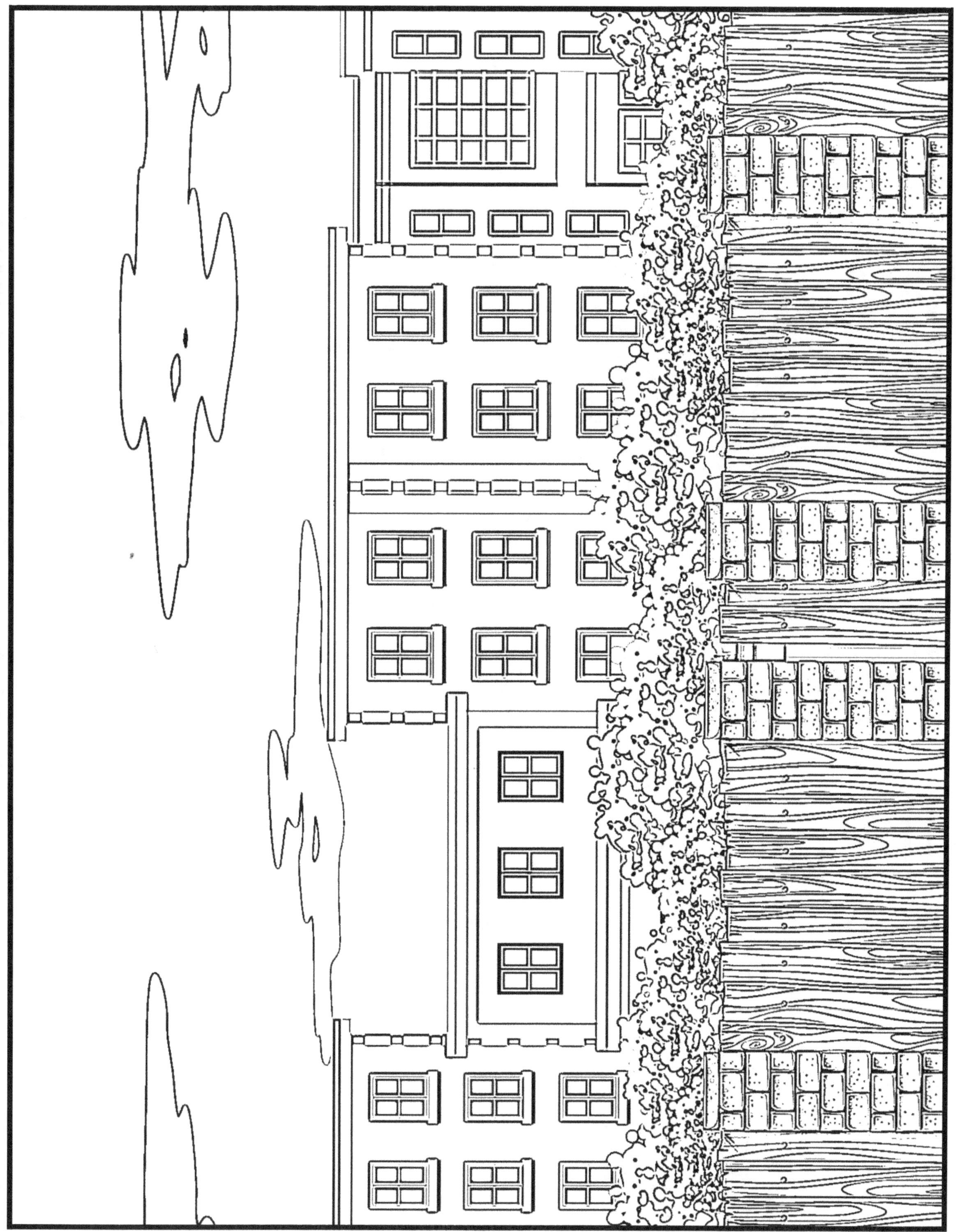

TELEPHONE

TELEPHONE

TELEPHONE

Habana

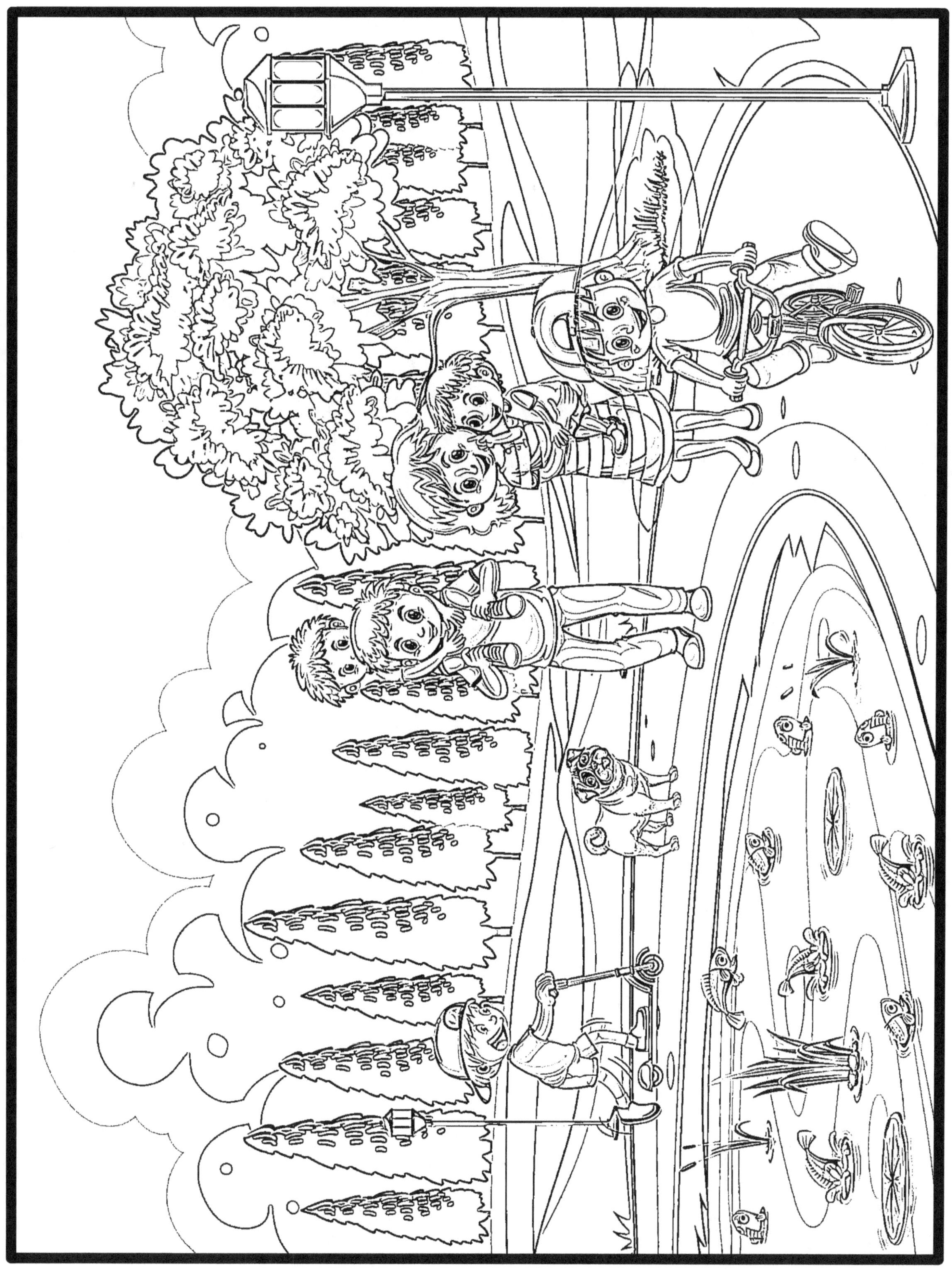

TELEPHONE